An African elephant's feet are so big we could only fit two **LIFESIZE** toenails on this page! Get your toes out and see who has the biggest toenails, you or an African elephant?

First American Edition 2018
Kane Miller, A Division of EDC Publishing

First published in Great Britain 2018 by Red Shed, an imprint of Egmont UK Limited.
Text and illustrations copyright © Sophy Henn 2018
Consultancy by John Woodward.

LIFESIZE

Sophy Henn

Kane Miller
A DIVISION OF EDC PUBLISHING

There are so many wonderful creatures on this planet, from the teeny tiny to the utterly **GIGANTIC**. But just how teeny tiny or utterly gigantic are they?

Well, in this book you can see for yourself, because every time you see the word **LIFESIZE** you will know you are looking at an animal, or part of an animal, that is actual size. For real!

So let's go on a **LIFESIZE** adventure,
and see how you measure up against some
of the world's most amazing animals. . .

Here is a **LIFESIZE** bee hummingbird. Isn't it tiny?
In fact, it's the world's smallest bird and it can beat
its wings a super-speedy 80 times per second.
Try flapping your arms that fast!

High-five a polar bear! Put your paw on the polar bear's **LIFESIZE** paw – whose is the biggest?

Polar bears live in a place called the Arctic, which is rather chilly! **BRRRRRR! HUGE** paws help spread their weight on the snow and ice.

Who else lives here?

A narwhal's tusk is actually a tooth that grows through its top lip. Ouch! It can be over 8 feet long.

These **LIFESIZE** lampreys have 11 to 12 rows of teeth. That's a lot of brushing before bedtime!

Try on a **LIFESIZE** toco toucan's beak. Hold it up to the side of your nose. How does it look?

The **toco toucan** lives in the hot, leafy forests of Cuba. Its super-snazzy beak makes up one third of its total size. That's like you having a beak that's half as tall as you are!

What other birds live in Cuba's forests?

Cuban parakeets are really sociable. This **LIFESIZE** parakeet is enjoying the shade and looking for some parakeet friends to play with.

Look! A flamboyance of flamingoes!

Aren't these **LIFESIZE** todies pretty? Their bright feathers aren't just for show, they are for camouflage in the colorful Cuban forests.

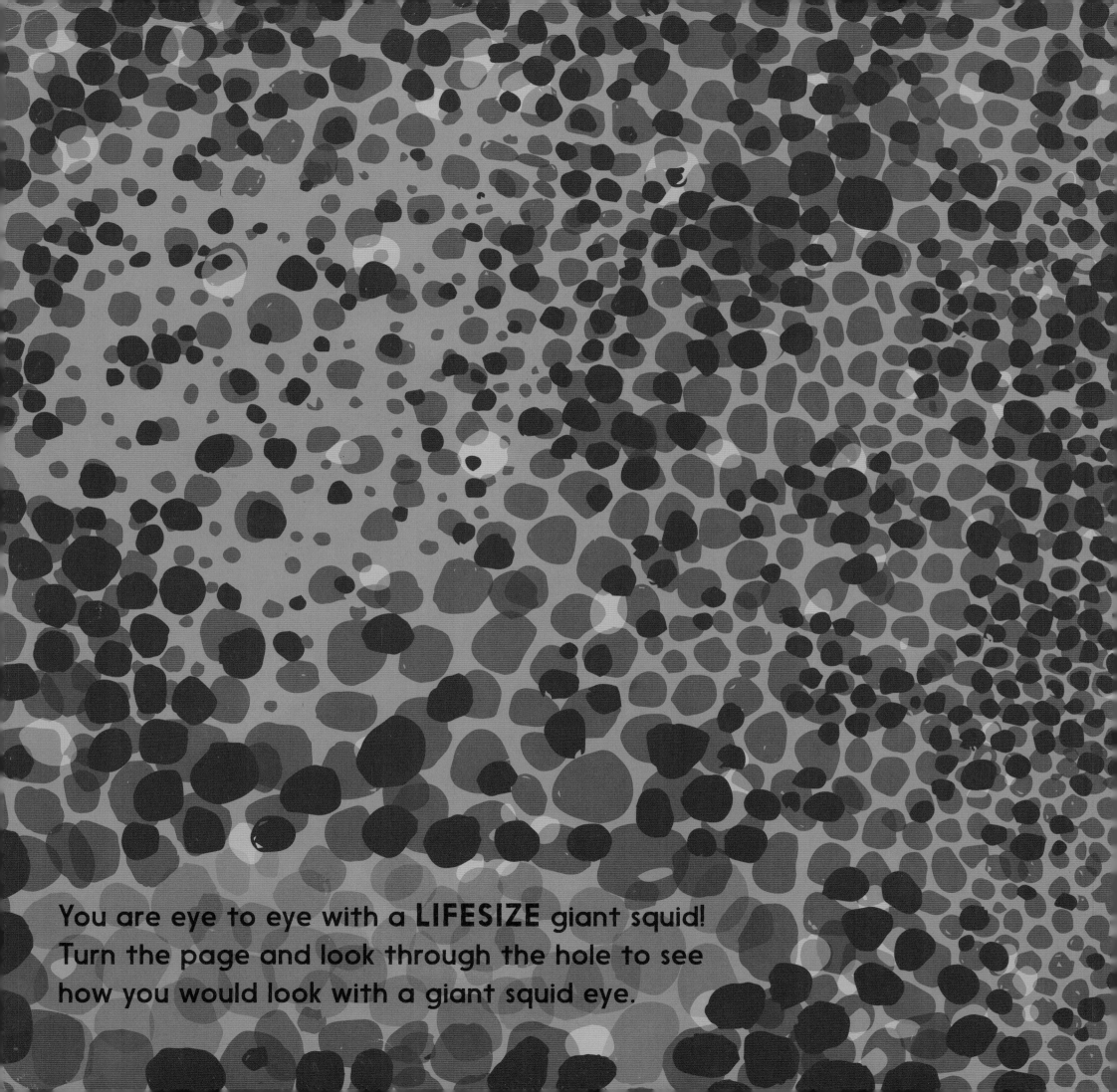

You are eye to eye with a **LIFESIZE** giant squid!
Turn the page and look through the hole to see
how you would look with a giant squid eye.

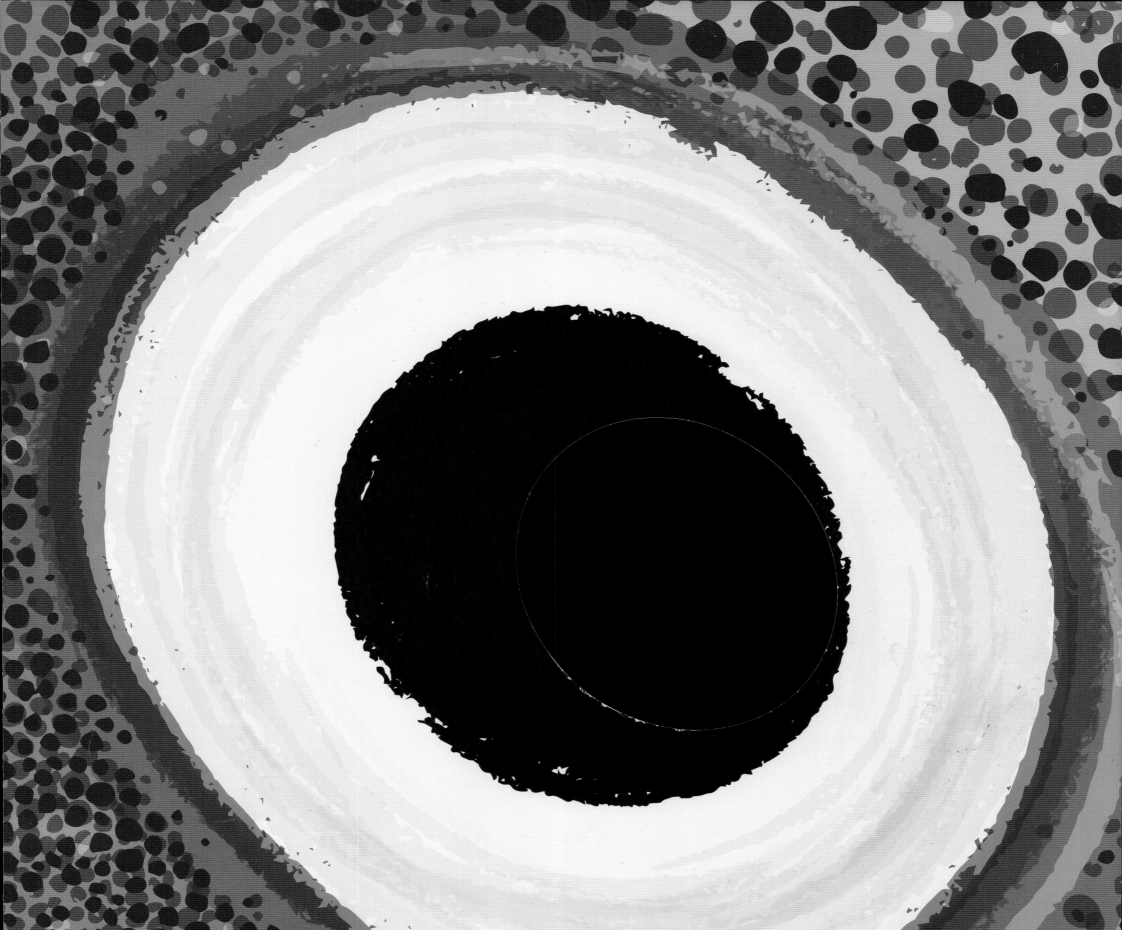

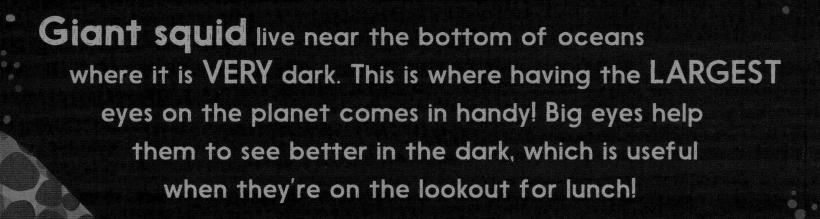

Giant squid live near the bottom of oceans where it is VERY dark. This is where having the LARGEST eyes on the planet comes in handy! Big eyes help them to see better in the dark, which is useful when they're on the lookout for lunch!

Who else lives down here?

Irukandji jellyfish are the smallest jellyfish in the world. They glow in the dark, just like the giant squid. But don't let the tiny twinkliness of this LIFESIZE jellyfish fool you, it has a powerful sting!

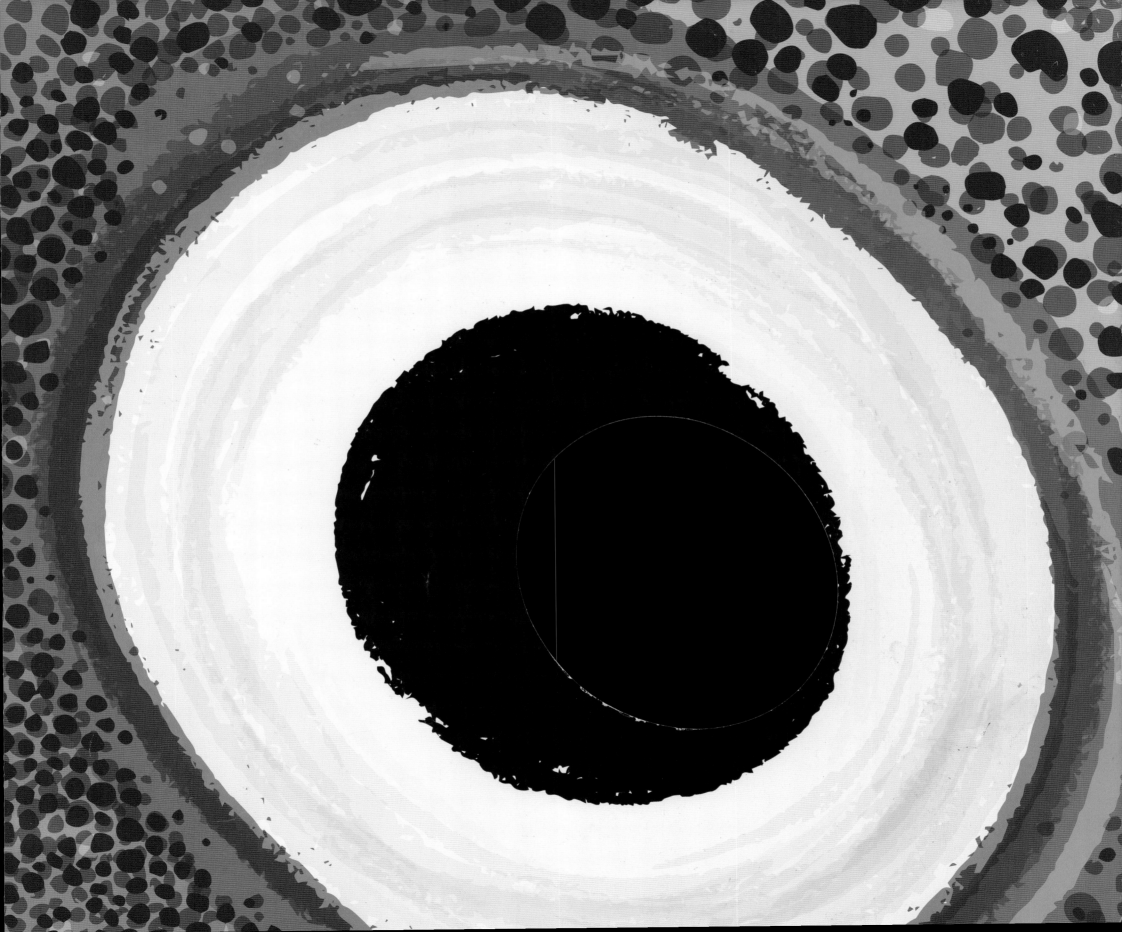

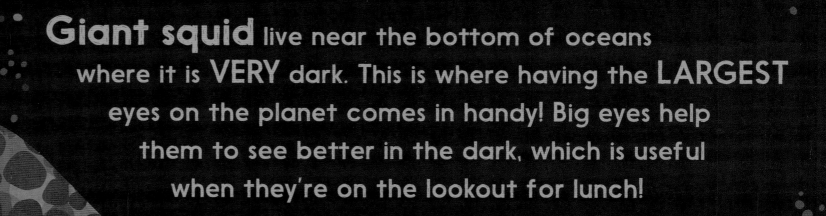

Giant squid live near the bottom of oceans where it is VERY dark. This is where having the LARGEST eyes on the planet comes in handy! Big eyes help them to see better in the dark, which is useful when they're on the lookout for lunch!

Who else lives down here?

Irukandji jellyfish are the smallest jellyfish in the world. They glow in the dark, just like the giant squid. But don't let the tiny twinkliness of this **LIFESIZE** jellyfish fool you, it has a powerful sting!

This **LIFESIZE** pea crab is tiny! Although he is only .2 inches wide, he has 10 legs. That's eight more than you!

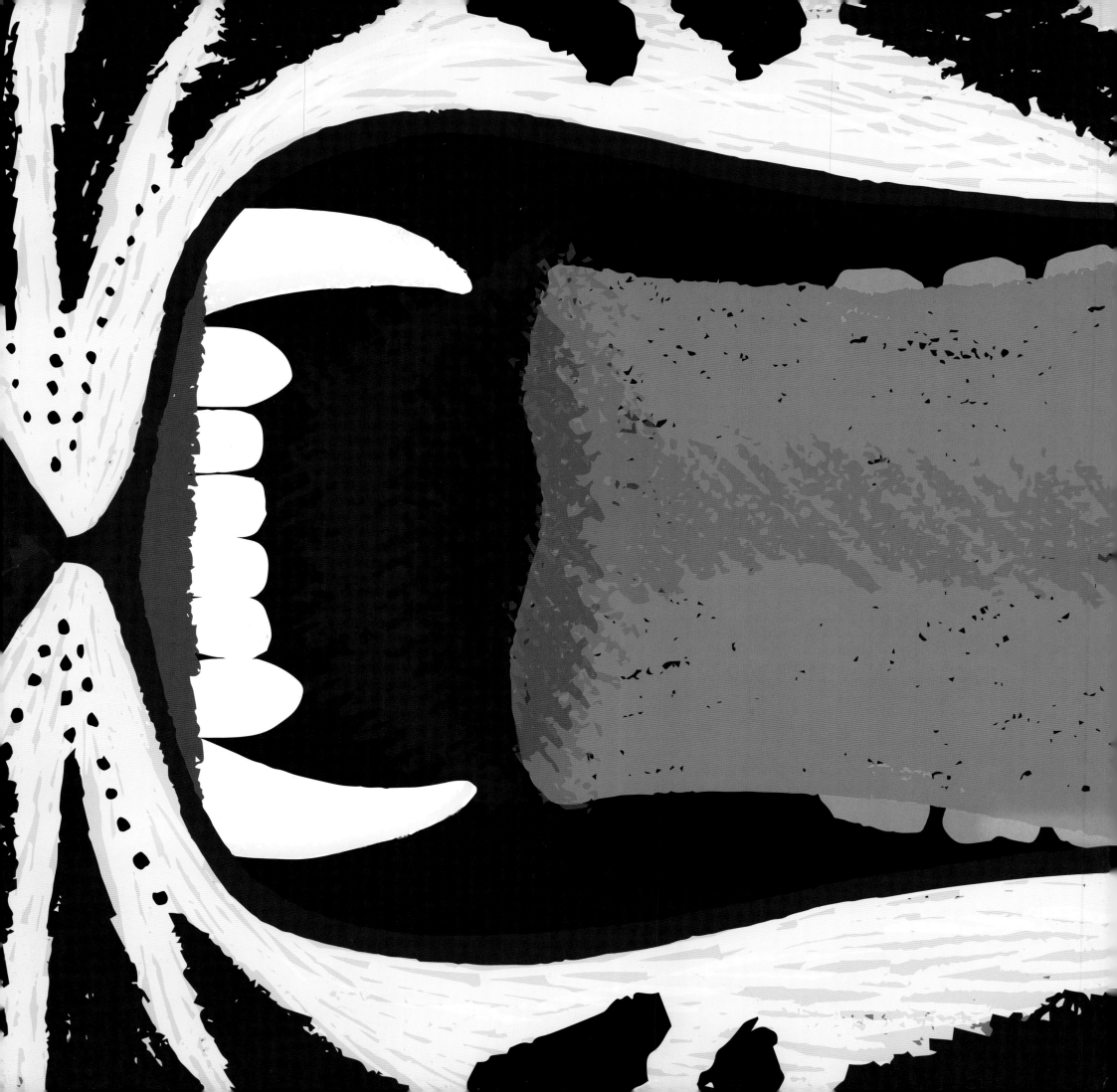

ROOOAAAARRR like a Bengal tiger!
Hold the book under your nose
to see what you would look like
with a **LIFESIZE** tiger roar.

Most **Bengal tigers** live in the vast forests of India. But it's easy for them to stay in touch as their roars can be heard up to two miles away. Pardon?

What other animals can you spot?

This is a **LIFESIZE** tiger centipede. These creatures have so many legs that they are bound to lose one here or there. But don't worry, they can just grow another!

Gray langur monkeys and
chital deer are great friends, warning
each other if there are any predators coming.
LOOK OUT FOR THE TIGER!

Here is a leaf . . .   . . . not really, it's a **LIFESIZE** leaf insect!
These clever insects pretend to be leaves
so they can hide from predators. Sneaky!

Stick your tongue out at a **LIFESIZE** giraffe!
Whose tongue is the longest?

African elephants are the largest land animals on the planet. They also have the biggest ears, which they flap to keep cool.

Cheetahs are completely dotty. No really, they each have up to 3,000 spots!

Giraffes live on the hot, grassy plains of Africa. They are the world's **TALLEST** animal so it makes sense that they have an extraordinarily long tongue. This helps them reach the leaves on acacia trees. Yum!

What other animals live here?

This **LIFESIZE** male rainbow lizard is usually reddish-brown, but it turns rainbow colored to impress female lizards.

Try these **LIFESIZE** kangaroo ears on for size.
Hold them up to your forehead and jump around
a bit. You are practically a kangaroo!

The fancy frill-necked lizard opens its mouth and pushes out its frill to scare away other animals. Boo!

Red kangaroos live in the hot and dusty Australian outback. Their big, pointy ears can swivel to pick up sounds from all around.

What other creatures live here?

To get out of the hot sun, this **LIFESIZE** desert scorpion can burrow up to three feet down in a twirly spiral. Phew!

Giant squid

Tentacle tip to tail: up to 60 feet

Did you know? A giant squid has eight arms and two tentacles. If a giant squid loses an arm, it just grows another one.

Wow! We've traveled the world and seen some amazing **LIFESIZE** animals. Let's see how these animals compare in size to one another.

Giraffe

Head to toe: up to 18 feet

Did you know? A group of giraffes is called a tower.

African elephant

Head to toe: up to 13 feet

Did you know? Elephant tusks are extra-long front (incisor) teeth.

Bengal tiger

Head to tail: up to 8.8 feet

Did you know? Every tiger has its own unique stripes – no two tigers are the same!

60 LIFESIZE books

18 LIFESIZE books

13 LIFESIZE books

9 LIFESIZE books

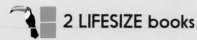 **2 LIFESIZE books**

Toco toucan

Beak to tail: up to 24 inches
The beak alone is 7.5 inches!

Did you know? Toucans rest their beaks
on their backs when they sleep.

Bee hummingbird

Head to tail: up to 2.4 inches

Did you know? Hummingbirds lick
sweet nectar out of flowers and
can lick up to 13 times per second!

Where do you fit into the lineup?
Measure yourself using this book to
see how you compare. Are you utterly
GIGANTIC or teeny tiny? Try measuring
your friends and family as well!

Polar bear

Head to toe: up to 8.2 feet

Did you know? Polar bears have
an amazing sense of smell and can
smell prey up to 10 miles away.

Red kangaroo

Height: up to 5 feet

Did you know? A male is called
a boomer, a female is called a
flyer and a baby is called a joey.

Giant panda

Head to tail: up to 5 feet

Did you know? Pandas spend up
to 12 hours eating every day.

 **8 LIFESIZE books**

 5 LIFESIZE books

 **5 LIFESIZE books**